Write to Dream

What does your FUTURE look like?

By Brad Killmeyer

Write to Dream

A Brad Killmeyer Book
Copyright © 2015, **Formulate Your Future, LLC.**
All rights reserved.

Writing & Publishing Process by PlugAndPlayPublishing.com
Book Cover by Tom Collins | www.TomsDesignFarm.com
Edited by Jenny Butterfield

ISBN: 1516802411
EAN-13: 978-1516802418

Disclaimer:

I dedicate this journal to my grandfather and grandmother, Russell and Eleanor Sosman. They have supplied me with a tremendous amount of support and encouragement in my life. Thank you both so much, without you this journal would not have been possible.

Russell Sosman Jan 5th 1934 — October 2nd 2010

I also want to thank my mother and father along with my soon-to-be-wife Nicole. I am so thankful to have each of you in my life.

Write to Dream
Table of Contents

"You will never change your life until you change something you do daily. The secret of your success is found in your daily routine."

John Maxwell

Your Dreams Start Here!

This journal is for dreamers, high achievers, and for people that are looking for a change. Like an airplane that gets you to your destination faster, this journal will help you reach your goals faster. You will avoid traffic, stop lights, and slow speed limits.

Using this journal does not mean you will not have challenges. There will be turbulence and you will have to fly through multiple storms, but with this journal, you will have the ability to overcome any challenge.

Unlike other journals, this journal is not simply about recording the day's events but provides you with an easy-to-follow routine which lays the foundation for success. In the end, you will not get a grade, you will get results.

Writing in your journal every day will help you become the successful person you are meant to be. You will accomplish this by:

- Setting goals
- Focusing on what is important
- Thinking positively
- Appreciating what you have in life
- Capturing timeless memories
- And much more!

The Morning: 3-2-1, Go Go Go

Your alarm goes off for the third time. You glance into the

bright light of your cell phone with one eye half open to discover you are going to be late. Immediately, you jump out of bed, take a lightening-fast shower, and quickly brush your teeth, all while attempting to find clothes to wear. You rinse your mouth out and finally find your shoes. Then you sprint out the door and get straight on the bus. All you really have time to do is hope that you didn't leave something important at home.

In another scenario, you could get up an hour early, go for a run, read for 20 minutes, and eat a full breakfast.

This journal is a balance between these two extremes. Invest a few minutes in yourself each morning. You are worth it!

During this time, you will start your day off on the right foot, set goals, and prioritize your day.

3 Steps to Starting Your Journal

Before you get started with your journal, I'd like to give you three steps that will help you avoid frustration and allow you to be successful with your journal.

Step 1: Create goals
Goals generate a vision of what you want your life to become. To be blunt, you must know what you want! Things will not just work out. Knowing what you want to accomplish is essential. This journal will ensure that you have set goals for each day before you leave the house.

Step 2: Make a commitment to yourself
On page 33, I've created a "Commitment Contract" for you to

fill out. Filling out this contract means that you are fully invested and agreeing to act by taking the time to journal each day. If you make this commitment, you will see results you want in as little as one week.

Step 3: Write in your journal each and every day
On the next two pages, I've given you "sample pages" of your journal, so you can see the five sections you'll be filling out.

On the sample pages to follow, you'll find some important details that explain each of the five sections, how to fill out that area, and why those areas are important to you and your success.

Writing in your journal each and every day will help you stay focused and motivated, as well as help you achieve more than you ever thought possible!

Share your journal with someone!

By sharing your journal with someone you will:
- Experience success faster
- Stay focused
- Be more likely to achieve your dreams

SAMPLE PAGES

I Am Thankful For:

1. _____   4. _____

2. _____   5. _____

3. _____   6. _____

What Would Make Today Successful?

☐ _____

☐ _____

☐ _____

Daily Affirmation...

I Feel Happy, I Feel Healthy, I Feel Terrific

I Feel Happy, I Feel Healthy, I Feel Terrific

I Feel Happy, I Feel Healthy, I Feel Terrific

I Am Ready For Today!

A.M. Section

In your journal, the left-hand pages are "A.M." pages and should be filled out each morning before you start your day.

SAMPLE PAGES

3 Positive Things That Happened Today:

1. _____

2. _____

3. _____

Capture a Timeless Memory:

_____

_____

_____

_____

_____

_____

_____

P.M. Section

In your journal, the right-hand pages are "P.M." pages and should be filled out each night before you end your day.

---

*"You can live a day in your life,
or you can put life in your day."*

Brad Killmeyer

How to Use Your Journal
A.M. Section

What am I thankful for?

When I was 15 years old, my mom arrived home from work and opened the garage door to enter the house. Immediately I said, "Mom, you wouldn't believe what was on Cribs today (a half hour show on MTV that showcased celebrity homes). I want a massive, heated swimming pool with waterfalls and a water slide, a showroom for my two new Bentley's, and a shower the size of our neighbors house."

My mom and dad worked hard and have provided so much for me. How do you think they felt when I asked for these things? Why don't we have a hot tub, a pizza oven, and an exotic car? Mom set me straight. She said, "I am happy you are dreaming big, and I hope one day get it all. Work hard and buy whatever you want with your money." That week, I bought a Rice Krispie treat and a movie ticket.

Now, what if instead of expressing envy , I expressed gratitude when my mom returned from work. I may have said, "Mom, thank you for working hard so that I do not have to worry about the bills." "Mom, thank you for getting up at 4 a.m. to get me an X-Box when it was released." "Mom, thank you for giving me a car to drive when I turned sixteen." "Mom, thank you for always believing in me and encouraging me to follow my dreams." "Mom, I love you! How was your day?"

How would those comments have made my mother feel? Can you see the difference?

You can make yourself feel great every morning by training yourself to be thankful for what you have in life. As soon as you wake up each morning, write down three things you are thankful for. Here are a few examples:

I Am Thankful For:
1. Being able to laugh at myself.
2. My ability to think on my feet.
3. The opportunity to positively influence others.

I Am Thankful For:
1. Being Tall.
2. Having a laptop computer.
3. Having excellent communication skills.

If you are struggling with what to be thankful for, here are some ideas for you:

- Family
- Friends
- Health
- Laughter
- Job
- Car
- Technology
- Food
- Computer
- Ice cream
- Online shopping
- Steak
- Air conditioning
- Fresh Fruit

Maybe you have too many ideas and don't need help finding things to be thankful for. After writing three examples, write down any others thoughts in the margins. It is okay to be thankful for the same things every morning. The important part is that you give thanks each morning. This exercise will help put you in a good mood to start your day.

What would make today successful?

The purpose of this section is to create goals. Setting goals will keep you on track and allow you to measure what you achieved each day. You will set three goals each day. It is significant to write your goals in the order of importance.

For example:
#1 is the top priority of the day
#2 second
#3 third

Your number three priority may be the hardest to select because you have several other priorities and find choosing difficult. You have to make a choice. Why? Because if you consistently complete your top three priorities each day, you will complete 21 goals in a week, 90 goals a month, and 1000 + goals in a year.

Take a deep breath! Think about how your life could be been different if you complete over 1000 of your top goals in the next year.

Example Goals:

What would make today successful?

☐ Give someone a compliment

☐ Add humor to your day listen to comedy for 15 minutes

☐ Apply to three college scholarships

What would make today successful?

☐ Go to Zumba or exercise

☐ Call your best friend

☐ Identify 3 volunteer opportunities

Daily Affirmation

I Feel Happy, I Feel Healthy, I Feel Terrific
I Feel Happy, I Feel Healthy, I Feel Terrific
I Feel Happy, I Feel Healthy, I Feel Terrific
I Am Ready For Today!

King Soloman, author of ancient Hebrew Wisdom Literature, wrote, "The tongue has the power of life and death." In other words, you have ability to affect the mood of others with how you speak. This means you have the power to influence yourself with words as well.

An affirmation is a statement that is declared to be true. Overtime, these statements can make a permanent change in your life. In the morning section, you will say this positive affirmation statement out loud three times: "I Feel Happy, I Feel Healthy, I Feel Terrific... I Am Ready For Today!" This statement will ensure that you leave the house motivated, feeling good, and ready to tackle your day.

When saying this affirmation statement, start at a normal voice level and get louder each time. Feel free to repeat this affirmation more than three times for an enhanced effect. Now, when you yell this, please do not wake up the whole neighborhood.

Even though that kind of enthusiasm would make me happy, I do not want to receive angry phone calls from parents. I do, however, want you to be successful. Be enthusiastic! Get loud! Be consistent! This practice is like a muscle. The more you exercise and use your affirmation, the more powerful it will become.

In the back of this book on page 91, there is a list of additional positive affirmation statements that I use in my own life. Read the statements if you want to increase the amount of positivity in your life.

"If you can't fly then run, if you can't run then walk, if you can't walk then crawl, but whatever you do you have to keep moving forward."

Martin Luther King Jr.

How to Use Your Journal
P.M. Section

The purpose of the P.M. portion of the day is to:

- Measure your success
- Keep a positive attitude by seeing progress
- Capture a timeless memory

In sports, we keep score to know who is winning. Reflecting on your progress allows you to keep score and measure your success. There is a box to the left of each goal in the morning section for you to evaluate your progress. Once you have completed a goal, place a "checkmark" in the box.

Example:

Before evaluation:

☐ Give someone a complement

☐ Listen to comedy for 15 minutes to laugh

☐ Apply for three college scholarships

After Evaluation:

 Give someone a complement

 Listen to comedy for 15 minutes to laugh

 Apply for three college scholarships

Your "checkmarks" show that you completed all three tasks. Excellent work! This is what you want every day.

Now you may have a day that looks like this:

 Give someone a complement

 Listen to comedy for 15 minutes to laugh

☐ Apply for three college scholarships

Nice job on getting two of the three tasks accomplished!

When you only accomplish two tasks:
First, decide if the unattained goal is still important. If the unattained goal is not important, then strike it from your list.

If the unattained goal is important, then decide if the goal needs to be modified, changed, or updated.

Finally, consider writing today's unattained goal as a top priority for tomorrow.

Evaluating your day will help hold you accountable, which will increase your productivity. Even if you only achieve one or two tasks you are still moving towards your goals.

Positive things that happened today

Right now, whether you are the most optimistic person in the world or struggling to find anything encouraging, this section will strengthen your positive attitude.

Inevitably, you will face demanding challenges, have set backs, and your mental toughness will be tested. A positive attitude will help you persevere through these times.

What to do? Write three positive aspects of your day.

Examples:

3 Positive Things That Happened Today:
1. I made it to school on time (not always easy)
2. I got a promotion at work
3. I hired a college admissions coach

3 Positive Things That Happened Today:
1. I got a date to Homecoming
2. I completed a bonus assignment for English
3. We won four straight football games

Be positive! Be Confident! Believe in Yourself!

Capture a Timeless Memory

By "Capture a Timeless Memory", I mean that you should paint a picture of a conversation, write about something you learned, or tell a story about event that stuck out in your day. Overtime, you will have an abundance of timeless memories.

"You have to be able to love yourself because that's when things fall into place."

Vanessa Hudgens

Bonus Tip:
Highlight Your Highlights

To get the most out of this journal, take a highlighter and high-light exceptional accomplishments, timeless memories, and positive aspects of your day. This will create an easy way to reference these accomplishments.

The next six pages contain three examples of what a completed day will look like in your journal. If you are ever not sure what to do, please refer back to these pages.

EXAMPLE PAGES

I Am Thankful For:

1. Inspirational people like Walt Disney
2. Being able to make the right decision even when it is hard
3. Having the internet

What Would Make Today Successful?

☑ Drink eight glasses of water

☑ Apply to a summer job

☐ Watch a movie with popcorn before bed to de-stress

Daily Affirmation...

I Feel Happy, I Feel Healthy, I Feel Terrific
I Feel Happy, I Feel Healthy, I Feel Terrific
I Feel Happy, I Feel Healthy, I Feel Terrific
I Am Ready For Today!

EXAMPLE PAGES

3 Positive Things That Happened Today:

1. I got a new cell phone
2. I got tipped $50 at work
3. My crush is in my science group (guess I will not miss a day this semester)

Capture a Timeless Memory:

One of my best friends, Ben, and I bought tickets to see the Pittsburgh Penguins play Game 7 against the Red Wings in Detroit. The Pens won 2-1, and we got to see our team win the Stanley Cup.

One of the most memorable parts was a guy from Detroit kept making fun Ben's cargo shorts. We were dying with laughter saying, "Dude, since when did cargo shorts go out of style?" Also Ben was so stressed in the final minutes of the game, he didn't even watch.

EXAMPLE PAGES

I Am Thankful For:

1. Choosing great friends

2. Being able to spend my life with Nicole

3. Having the ability to positively influence today's youth

What Would Make Today Successful?

- ☑ Run three miles
- ☑ Read for 30 minutes
- ☑ Go to a network event tonight

Daily Affirmation...

I Feel Happy, I Feel Healthy, I Feel Terrific

I Feel Happy, I Feel Healthy, I Feel Terrific

I Feel Happy, I Feel Healthy, I Feel Terrific

I Am Ready For Today!

EXAMPLE PAGES

3 Positive Things That Happened Today:

1. I ran three miles
2. I met six new people at the networking event
3. I talked to my grandmother for over thirty minutes on the phone

Capture a Timeless Memory:

My mom was at a training class in Michigan. The second half of the class was laid back and very casual. So casual, that one young man wore a shirt that said, "They didn't hire me for my attitude." Haha, that is hilarious. I would never wear that to a work function.

EXAMPLE PAGES

I Am Thankful For:

1. Having a good sense of humor
2. Being able to study abroad in Italy
3. Spell check on computers

What Would Make Today Successful?

☐ Go to the high school basketball game as a break from studying my physics

☐ Schedule a day to job shadow at the local law office

☐ Sign up for a club at school

Daily Affirmation...

I Feel Happy, I Feel Healthy, I Feel Terrific
I Feel Happy, I Feel Healthy, I Feel Terrific
I Feel Happy, I Feel Healthy, I Feel Terrific
I Am Ready For Today!

EXAMPLE PAGES

3 Positive Things That Happened Today:

1. Two students I coach said they appreciate how much I care about their success
2. I posted this quote to Facebook: "I may not be there yet, but I am closer than I was yesterday."
3. I had dinner with Nicole (turned my phone off while we ate, scored major points)

Capture a Timeless Memory:

I mentor two businesses for Entrepreneuring Youth. Entrepreneuring Youth is an organization that helps young people start and operate businesses as a way to guide them toward their own career paths. Kaleb and Maddie make cannoli's, and Derek makes all natural granola bars. Tonight was their final presentations. I was so proud of them all year. Words can't describe the emotions that I felt when Derek's name was called for third place, winning $1,000, and then moments later, Kaleb and Maddie won first place and were awarded $1,500. I was able to see them celebrate with their families. Tonight was very special.

"It's time to make a commitment and start investing in yourself each and every day."

Brad Killmeyer

Time to Commit
to Greatness

It's time to make a commitment and start investing in yourself each and every day by filling out your journal. Again, writing in your journal will help you set goals, prioritize, and strengthen your positive attitude.

On the next two pages, you'll find an example of a "Commitment Contract" for you to model, as well as a fill-in-the-blank Commitment Contract for you to fill out.

Commitment Contract
Example

I, Brad Killmeyer, commit to writing in this journal for at a minimum seven days straight, beginning March 11th.

Writing in this journal is very important to me because,

- I want to live a positive life
- I want to create an overflow of happiness in my life
- I need a tool to help keep me focused each day on what is most important

When I finish seven straight days of writing in this journal, I will reward myself by going to dinner at my favorite restaurant.

If I fall short and don't write seven straight days, I will shake it off and start another seven days.

What two tips will you use to help ensure that you will write in your journal every day? Check off the two tips that you believe will be most helpful to you.

☐ Keep your journal in the same place everyday

☐ Write in your journal before you get ready for bed

☐ Write the morning portion of your journal before you take a shower

☐ Share your intention with this journal with someone you trust

Signature: Brad Killmeyer

Commitment Contract

I, _Jeremy_____, commit to writing in this journal for at a minimum seven days straight, beginning _march 4_____.

Writing in this journal is very important to me because,
- better myself
- outside Box thinker
- to learn

When I finish seven straight days of writing in this journal, I will reward myself with _____
_____.

If I fall short and don't write seven straight days, I will
_____
_____.

What two tips will you use to help ensure that you will write in your journal every day? Check off the two tips that you believe will be most helpful to you.

☑ Keep your journal in the same place everyday

☑ Write in your journal before you get ready for bed

☐ Write the morning portion of your journal before you take a shower

☐ Share your intention with this journal with someone you trust

Signature: _Jenny Linew_____

"You have everything you need
to be successful."

Brad Killmeyer

Your "Write to Dream" Starts on the Next Page

Now that you know how to fill out the journal pages, and you're committed to writing in your journal each and every day, it's time to get started.

Day 1 of your journal starts on the next page.

I'm so excited for you to see what happens over the next 21 days. Stay on track, and have fun!

Date: ___ / ___ / _____

"Strive for Greatness"

I Am Thankful For:

1. _____   4. _____
2. _____   5. _____
3. _____   6. _____

What Would Make Today Successful?

☐ _____

☐ _____

☐ _____

Daily Affirmation...

I Feel Happy, I Feel Healthy, I Feel Terrific
I Feel Happy, I Feel Healthy, I Feel Terrific
I Feel Happy, I Feel Healthy, I Feel Terrific
I Am Ready For Today!

3 Positive Things That Happened Today:

1. _____
2. _____
3. _____

Capture a Timeless Memory:

_____

_____

_____

_____

_____

_____

_____

_____

_____

_____

Date: ___ / ___ / _____

"Embrace Change"

I Am Thankful For:

1. _____   4. _____
2. _____   5. _____
3. _____   6. _____

What Would Make Today Successful?

☐ _____

☐ _____

☐ _____

Daily Affirmation...

I Feel Happy, I Feel Healthy, I Feel Terrific

I Feel Happy, I Feel Healthy, I Feel Terrific

I Feel Happy, I Feel Healthy, I Feel Terrific

I Am Ready For Today!

3 Positive Things That Happened Today:

1. _____
2. _____
3. _____

Capture a Timeless Memory:

_____

_____

_____

_____

_____

_____

_____

_____

_____

_____

_____

Date: ___ / ___ / _____

"Give Your Best Today"

I Am Thankful For:

1. _____   4. _____
2. _____   5. _____
3. _____   6. _____

What Would Make Today Successful?

☐ _____

☐ _____

☐ _____

Daily Affirmation...

I Feel Happy, I Feel Healthy, I Feel Terrific
I Feel Happy, I Feel Healthy, I Feel Terrific
I Feel Happy, I Feel Healthy, I Feel Terrific
I Am Ready For Today!

3 Positive Things That Happened Today:

1. _____
2. _____
3. _____

Capture a Timeless Memory:

_____

_____

_____

_____

_____

_____

_____

_____

_____

_____

Date: ___ / ___ / _____

"Celebrate Your Accomplishments"

I Am Thankful For:

1. _____   4. _____
2. _____   5. _____
3. _____   6. _____

What Would Make Today Successful?

☐ _____

☐ _____

☐ _____

Daily Affirmation...

I Feel Happy, I Feel Healthy, I Feel Terrific
I Feel Happy, I Feel Healthy, I Feel Terrific
I Feel Happy, I Feel Healthy, I Feel Terrific
I Am Ready For Today!

3 Positive Things That Happened Today:

1. _____
2. _____
3. _____

Capture a Timeless Memory:

_____

_____

_____

_____

_____

_____

_____

_____

_____

_____

_____

Date: ___ / ___ / _____

"Stay Focused"

I Am Thankful For:

1. _____ 4. _____
2. _____ 5. _____
3. _____ 6. _____

What Would Make Today Successful?

☐ _____

☐ _____

☐ _____

Daily Affirmation...

I Feel Happy, I Feel Healthy, I Feel Terrific
I Feel Happy, I Feel Healthy, I Feel Terrific
I Feel Happy, I Feel Healthy, I Feel Terrific
I Am Ready For Today!

3 Positive Things That Happened Today:

1. _____
2. _____
3. _____

Capture a Timeless Memory:

_____

_____

_____

_____

_____

_____

_____

_____

_____

_____

_____

Date: ___ / ___ / _____
"Dream Big"

I Am Thankful For:

1. _____   4. _____
2. _____   5. _____
3. _____   6. _____

What Would Make Today Successful?

☐ _____

☐ _____

☐ _____

Daily Affirmation...

I Feel Happy, I Feel Healthy, I Feel Terrific
I Feel Happy, I Feel Healthy, I Feel Terrific
I Feel Happy, I Feel Healthy, I Feel Terrific
I Am Ready For Today!

3 Positive Things That Happened Today:

1. _____
2. _____
3. _____

Capture a Timeless Memory:

_____

_____

_____

_____

_____

_____

_____

_____

_____

_____

_____

Date: ___ / ___ / _____

"The Only Way You Do Not Succeed
Is If You Give Up"

I Am Thankful For:

1. _____   4. _____
2. _____   5. _____
3. _____   6. _____

What Would Make Today Successful?

☐ _____

☐ _____

☐ _____

Daily Affirmation...

I Feel Happy, I Feel Healthy, I Feel Terrific
I Feel Happy, I Feel Healthy, I Feel Terrific
I Feel Happy, I Feel Healthy, I Feel Terrific
I Am Ready For Today!

3 Positive Things That Happened Today:

1. _____
2. _____
3. _____

Capture a Timeless Memory:

_____

_____

_____

_____

_____

_____

_____

_____

_____

_____

_____

"I know for sure that what we dwell on is who we become."

Oprah Winfrey

Congratulations on Your First 7 Days!

Congratulations! You have written in your journal for one week. You have changed your life for the better.

You are setting and achieving your goals, prioritizing your day, thinking positively, and capturing timeless memories that will last a lifetime.

This powerful journal will help you take your life to places you never imagined. Keep up the great work!

Date: ___ / ___ / _____

"Laugh More"

I Am Thankful For:

1. _____   4. _____
2. _____   5. _____
3. _____   6. _____

What Would Make Today Successful?

☐ _____

☐ _____

☐ _____

Daily Affirmation...

I Feel Happy, I Feel Healthy, I Feel Terrific
I Feel Happy, I Feel Healthy, I Feel Terrific
I Feel Happy, I Feel Healthy, I Feel Terrific
I Am Ready For Today!

3 Positive Things That Happened Today:

1. _____
2. _____
3. _____

Capture a Timeless Memory:

_____

_____

_____

_____

_____

_____

_____

_____

_____

_____

_____

_____

Date: ___ / ___ / _____

"Always Believe In Yourself"

I Am Thankful For:

1. _____   4. _____
2. _____   5. _____
3. _____   6. _____

What Would Make Today Successful?

☐ _____

☐ _____

☐ _____

Daily Affirmation...

I Feel Happy, I Feel Healthy, I Feel Terrific
I Feel Happy, I Feel Healthy, I Feel Terrific
I Feel Happy, I Feel Healthy, I Feel Terrific
I Am Ready For Today!

3 Positive Things That Happened Today:

1. _____
2. _____
3. _____

Capture a Timeless Memory:

_____

_____

_____

_____

_____

_____

_____

_____

_____

_____

_____

Date: ___ / ___ / _____

"You Can Do Whatever You Put Your Mind To"

I Am Thankful For:

1. _____   4. _____
2. _____   5. _____
3. _____   6. _____

What Would Make Today Successful?

☐ _____

☐ _____

☐ _____

Daily Affirmation...

I Feel Happy, I Feel Healthy, I Feel Terrific
I Feel Happy, I Feel Healthy, I Feel Terrific
I Feel Happy, I Feel Healthy, I Feel Terrific
I Am Ready For Today!

3 Positive Things That Happened Today:

1. _____
2. _____
3. _____

Capture a Timeless Memory:

_____

_____

_____

_____

_____

_____

_____

_____

_____

_____

_____

Date: ___ / ___ / _____

"Do Not Be Afraid to Try Something New"

I Am Thankful For:

1. _____   4. _____

2. _____   5. _____

3. _____   6. _____

What Would Make Today Successful?

☐ _____

☐ _____

☐ _____

Daily Affirmation...

I Feel Happy, I Feel Healthy, I Feel Terrific

I Feel Happy, I Feel Healthy, I Feel Terrific

I Feel Happy, I Feel Healthy, I Feel Terrific

I Am Ready For Today!

3 Positive Things That Happened Today:

1. _____
2. _____
3. _____

Capture a Timeless Memory:

_____

_____

_____

_____

_____

_____

_____

_____

_____

_____

_____

Date: ___ / ___ / _____

"Be Fearless"

I Am Thankful For:

1. _____   4. _____
2. _____   5. _____
3. _____   6. _____

What Would Make Today Successful?

☐ _____

☐ _____

☐ _____

Daily Affirmation...

I Feel Happy, I Feel Healthy, I Feel Terrific
I Feel Happy, I Feel Healthy, I Feel Terrific
I Feel Happy, I Feel Healthy, I Feel Terrific
I Am Ready For Today!

3 Positive Things That Happened Today:

1. _____
2. _____
3. _____

Capture a Timeless Memory:

_____

_____

_____

_____

_____

_____

_____

_____

_____

_____

_____

Date: ___ / ___ / _____

"It Is Okay To Be Human"

I Am Thankful For:

1. _____   4. _____
2. _____   5. _____
3. _____   6. _____

What Would Make Today Successful?

☐ _____

☐ _____

☐ _____

Daily Affirmation...

I Feel Happy, I Feel Healthy, I Feel Terrific
I Feel Happy, I Feel Healthy, I Feel Terrific
I Feel Happy, I Feel Healthy, I Feel Terrific
I Am Ready For Today!

3 Positive Things That Happened Today:

1. _____
2. _____
3. _____

Capture a Timeless Memory:

_____

_____

_____

_____

_____

_____

_____

_____

_____

_____

_____

Date: ___ / ___ / _____

"Focus on the Good in Life"

I Am Thankful For:

1. _____   4. _____
2. _____   5. _____
3. _____   6. _____

What Would Make Today Successful?

☐ _____

☐ _____

☐ _____

Daily Affirmation...

I Feel Happy, I Feel Healthy, I Feel Terrific
I Feel Happy, I Feel Healthy, I Feel Terrific
I Feel Happy, I Feel Healthy, I Feel Terrific
I Am Ready For Today!

3 Positive Things That Happened Today:

1. _____
2. _____
3. _____

Capture a Timeless Memory:

_____

_____

_____

_____

_____

_____

_____

_____

_____

_____

"You must be the change that you wish to see in the world."

Gandhi

Congratulations on Your First 2 Weeks!

Congratulations! You have written in your journal for two weeks. How does it feel to have a positive attitude and be on track?

These two weeks are a just a preview of what you can achieve when using your journal. Keep writing!

Date: ___ / ___ / _____

"Be Confident"

I Am Thankful For:

1. _____   4. _____
2. _____   5. _____
3. _____   6. _____

What Would Make Today Successful?

☐ _____

☐ _____

☐ _____

Daily Affirmation...

I Feel Happy, I Feel Healthy, I Feel Terrific
I Feel Happy, I Feel Healthy, I Feel Terrific
I Feel Happy, I Feel Healthy, I Feel Terrific
I Am Ready For Today!

3 Positive Things That Happened Today:

1. _____
2. _____
3. _____

Capture a Timeless Memory:

_____

_____

_____

_____

_____

_____

_____

_____

_____

_____

Date: ___ / ___ / _____

"Success Is No Accident"

I Am Thankful For:

1. _____   4. _____

2. _____   5. _____

3. _____   6. _____

What Would Make Today Successful?

☐ _____

☐ _____

☐ _____

Daily Affirmation...

I Feel Happy, I Feel Healthy, I Feel Terrific

I Feel Happy, I Feel Healthy, I Feel Terrific

I Feel Happy, I Feel Healthy, I Feel Terrific

I Am Ready For Today!

3 Positive Things That Happened Today:

1. _____
2. _____
3. _____

Capture a Timeless Memory:

_____

_____

_____

_____

_____

_____

_____

_____

_____

_____

_____

Date: ___ / ___ / _____

"Everything Is Possible"

I Am Thankful For:

1. _____   4. _____
2. _____   5. _____
3. _____   6. _____

What Would Make Today Successful?

☐ _____

☐ _____

☐ _____

Daily Affirmation...

I Feel Happy, I Feel Healthy, I Feel Terrific
I Feel Happy, I Feel Healthy, I Feel Terrific
I Feel Happy, I Feel Healthy, I Feel Terrific
I Am Ready For Today!

3 Positive Things That Happened Today:

1. _____
2. _____
3. _____

Capture a Timeless Memory:

_____

_____

_____

_____

_____

_____

_____

_____

_____

_____

_____

Date: ___ / ___ / _____

"Dreams Do Not Work Unless You Do"

I Am Thankful For:

1. _____ 4. _____
2. _____ 5. _____
3. _____ 6. _____

What Would Make Today Successful?

☐ _____

☐ _____

☐ _____

Daily Affirmation...

I Feel Happy, I Feel Healthy, I Feel Terrific
I Feel Happy, I Feel Healthy, I Feel Terrific
I Feel Happy, I Feel Healthy, I Feel Terrific
I Am Ready For Today!

3 Positive Things That Happened Today:

1. _____
2. _____
3. _____

Capture a Timeless Memory:

_____

_____

_____

_____

_____

_____

_____

_____

_____

_____

Date: ___ / ___ / _____
"A Long Journey Begins with a Single Step"

I Am Thankful For:

1. _____   4. _____
2. _____   5. _____
3. _____   6. _____

What Would Make Today Successful?

☐ _____

☐ _____

☐ _____

Daily Affirmation...

I Feel Happy, I Feel Healthy, I Feel Terrific
I Feel Happy, I Feel Healthy, I Feel Terrific
I Feel Happy, I Feel Healthy, I Feel Terrific
I Am Ready For Today!

3 Positive Things That Happened Today:

1. _____
2. _____
3. _____

Capture a Timeless Memory:

_____

_____

_____

_____

_____

_____

_____

_____

_____

_____

_____

Date: ___ / ___ / _____

"Do Something Fun"

I Am Thankful For:

1. _____   4. _____
2. _____   5. _____
3. _____   6. _____

What Would Make Today Successful?

☐ _____

☐ _____

☐ _____

Daily Affirmation...

I Feel Happy, I Feel Healthy, I Feel Terrific
I Feel Happy, I Feel Healthy, I Feel Terrific
I Feel Happy, I Feel Healthy, I Feel Terrific
I Am Ready For Today!

3 Positive Things That Happened Today:

1. _____
2. _____
3. _____

Capture a Timeless Memory:

_____

_____

_____

_____

_____

_____

_____

_____

_____

_____

_____

Date: ___ / ___ / _____

"Inspire Others"

I Am Thankful For:

1. _____   4. _____
2. _____   5. _____
3. _____   6. _____

What Would Make Today Successful?

☐ _____

☐ _____

☐ _____

Daily Affirmation...

I Feel Happy, I Feel Healthy, I Feel Terrific
I Feel Happy, I Feel Healthy, I Feel Terrific
I Feel Happy, I Feel Healthy, I Feel Terrific
I Am Ready For Today!

3 Positive Things That Happened Today:

1. _____
2. _____
3. _____

Capture a Timeless Memory:

_____

_____

_____

_____

_____

_____

_____

_____

_____

_____

"All our dreams can come true, if we have the courage to pursue them."

Walt Disney

Congratulations on Finishing the Entire 21-Day Journal!

Congratulations! Your life will never be the same. By writing for 21 days in your journal, you have developed a routine that allows you to achieve your dreams. You are becoming the successful person you were meant to be.

You have changed your life forever for the better. I wish you a happy, healthy, terrific life.

-Brad Killmeyer

Bonus Chapter
7 Life Lessons to Be Happy in High School

1. Love Yourself

The key to a happy life is the acceptance of yourself. Have you ever:

- questioned yourself?
- thought you are not good enough?
- said to yourself, "Why am I so stupid?"

All of these statements teach your mind and body to believe these statements. The statements above are not helpful. Instead, love yourself. Answer these three questions.

What I love the most about myself is _____

_____.

I am most proud of myself for _____

_____.

The word that best describes me is _____.

#2 – Sleep is Serious

Benefits of Sleep

- Sharpen attention
- Improve memory
- Lower stress
- Improve grades
- Enhance performance in sports

Lack of sleep can negatively affect

- Concentration
- Memory
- Energy level
- And overall health

Getting the proper rest is tough. Especially when tests, projects, and after-school activities pile up. Here are three tips to get the sleep you need.

1. Avoid naps during the day
2. Practice good time management with your school work to avoid all-nighters
3. Go to bed and wake up at the same time each day

This allows your body to get in a routine. There will be exceptions, but the closer the better. Avoid sleeping until 2 p.m. on the weekends!!!

#3 Find a Career You Love

Let's do some simple math, so you can see how important it is to find a career you love. Let's say the average person works 10 hour days for 50 years :

- 5 days a week X 10 hours per day = 50 hours per week
- 50 hours per week X 50 weeks per year (*with 2 weeks vacation time*) = 2500 hours per year
- 50 years X 2500 hours per year = 125,000 hours
- 125,000 / 24 hours per day = 5208 full days of work
- 5208 days / 365 days per year = 14.3 YEARS of your life at work!

Spend your life doing something that you want to do! This decision is the second most important decision, second only to deciding who you want to spend your life with.

---

3 Tips to Finding Your Career

1. Job shadowing: Allows you to discover your interests and will help you avoid choosing a career that makes you unhappy.

2. Start early: It is never too soon to begin your search.

3. Do not get discouraged: It may take time to find what you love to do…Keep looking until you find what you love.

#4 - Find a way to De-Stress

We all get angry, and we all get stressed. When we get frustrated, this negativity effects our mood, our decisions, and we don't always make good choices. What are three ways that you can de-stress…

1.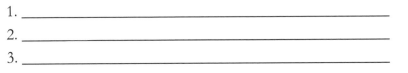

2. _____

3. _____

Here are some ideas:

- Read out loud the affirmation "I Feel Happy, I Feel Healthy, I Feel Terrific" (x3)

- Remind yourself what you are thankful for

- Identify your stress triggers

- Exercise
- Deep breathing
- Watch a funny video

#5 - Find a Hobby

Do something you love. I can't choose a hobby for you, but I do have a tip for you when you do find your hobby: No Cell Phone!

Focus on what you are doing. Everything else can wait. You will never find me on a golf course with a cell phone on.

#6 Choose Your Friends Wisely

The company you keep will be the person you become. Late in my sophomore year, I completely switched my friends because the group I was hanging with started to get into heavy drinking and drugs.

That choice was not easy, but making that change effected my life for the better. Two friends from the group I left died because of drugs and alcohol. But on the flip side of the coin, my two best friends in life to this day - and co-best men at my wedding - came from making the bold move to make new friends.

Here is the secret...
Become friends with people that:
- Help you become a better person
- Support you
- Are a positive influence

Do not be afraid to make a change. I did, and so can you!

#7 Formulate Your Future

Life will not always just fall into place. Make a plan for your future. While you are pursing your dreams, know that nothing will ever replace hard work, determination, and perseverance.

"We have the power to control our attitude, and that makes all the difference."

Brad Killmeyer

Additional Affirmation Statements

1. An abundance of unexpected opportunities are coming my way

2. I will accomplish whatever I set out to do

3. I believe in myself and my abilities

4. I choose happiness, success, and wealth in my life

5. I am stronger than any excuse, and I can overcome any challenge that I face

6. I am making things happen

7. I am confident, happy, and moving in the right direction

8. I am in charge of how I feel, and I feel awesome!

9. I am open to new ideas, I can adapt to any situation, I am a leader

10. I am fresh, focused and determined to reach my goals

11. I can be whatever I want to be, my future looks great!

"I consistently followed Brad's principals in <u>Write to Dream</u>. I set goals, prioritized my day, and kept a positive attitude. These teachings lead me to a first place award in a business competition, in which my partner and I won $1,500 to start our business."

Caleb
High School Student

About the Author

Brad Killmeyer was concurrently enrolled at the Community College of Allegheny County (CCAC) while still in high school. This proactive approach helped him earn an Economics degree from Washington and Jefferson College in just three years. After completing his undergraduate education, he spent three years in the financial services industry at Northwestern Mutual and Luttner Financial Group. This career allowed Brad to build rapport with many professionals and taught him essential skills on how to build a business.

Brad is now an inspirational, youth speaker and owner of Formulate Your Future, LLC. Brad helps high school students by sharing his personal story and experiences, including how he has overcome a major health issue.

Brad is an effective speaker because he is able to connect with students through the use of his stories and humor. If you want a speaker who will entertain and inspire your students, look no further than Brad Killmeyer.

You can learn more about Brad and how to reserve him for your next high school, college, or organizational event by visiting BradKillmeyer.com.

"<u>Write to Dream</u> holds students accountable for their actions, teaches time management, and makes sure that each day starts and ends in a positive way."

Kurt Mahan
Teacher, Brownsville High School, PA

Looking for a Speaker?

Today, students face a massive amount of peer pressure, more is expected of them than ever before, and they have to deal with countless distractions with social media and advertising.

After graduation, the intensity gets worse. Companies are more selective when hiring, and colleges are more competitive. Students can easily get overwhelmed or not understand the importance of their actions. Hearing Brad's story about overcoming challenges teaches students essential life lessons including:

- Teamwork & Accountability
- How to overcome challenges and use them to your advantage
- How to deal with judgment from others and how to not let it affect you
- Setting and reaching achievable goals
- Time management & making healthy choices

In addition, your students will know they are not alone when facing challenges and they will be encouraged to seek the help they need.

Last, your students will connect with Brad through the use of his stories, clean-humor, and his fun, contagious attitude!

**Book Brad Killmeyer today at
<u>BradKillmeyer.com/BookNow</u>!**

"<u>Write to Dream</u> is more than a journal,
it provides outstanding guidance and support
for students trying to reach their potential."

Angela
High School Student